Mastering Management Styles: Expert Guidance for Managers

Discover and perfect your ultimate management style
to succeed as a leader

Harris Silverman

Impackt Publishing
We Mean Business

Mastering Management Styles: Expert Guidance for Managers

First published: April 2014

Production Reference: 1020414

Published by Impackt Publishing Ltd.
Livery Place
35 Livery Street
Birmingham B3 2PB, UK.

ISBN 978-1-78300-046-3

www.Impacktpub.com

Cover Image by Zeeshan Chawdhary (imzeeshanc@gmail.com)

Credits

Author

Harris Silverman

Reviewers

Alasdair Dewar

Carol M. Heller

Project Coordinators

Venitha Cutinho

Hardik Patel

Commissioning Editor

Danielle Rosen

Copy Editors

Tanvi Bhatt

Ameesha Green

Paul Hindle

Faisal Siddiqui

Proofreaders

Simran Bhogal

Maria Gould

Ameesha Green

Paul Hindle

Cover Work

Melwyn D'sa

Production Coordinator

Melwyn D'sa

About the Author

Harris Silverman is a Management Coach and Career Counselor who works on the development of management skills, career planning, and career advancement with both corporations and individuals. He has extensive experience in employee development in both the public and private sectors, and holds an MBA and a Bachelor of Education degree, in addition to a BA.

He is available for consultation both by telephone and in person, worldwide. He is based in Toronto, Canada.

For more information about Harris and to read his blog, please visit www.HarrisSilverman.com.

About the Reviewers

Alasdair Dewar is a highly experienced manager with a vast wealth of industrial and management experience learned across a varied range of industries. Alasdair graduated from Napier University in Edinburgh, Scotland with an honors degree in Engineering Management in 1993. He has worked in electronics, FMCG, Pharma, and traditional manufacturing companies. Alasdair is happily married with three wonderful children, and now lives in Scotland with his family.

Carol M. Heller has more than 20 years of executive level management experience including P&L responsibility and managing large B2B sales, marketing and customer care organizations spanning multiple high technology segments, including telecom, content management and business outsourced software solutions both domestically and internationally. Carol has an outstanding record of consistently achieving defined objectives while creating and implementing effective sales and marketing strategies in challenging market environments. Her ability to lead and manage organizations in competitive environments has translated into market success for the corporate divisions she has led. She specializes in motivating and challenging the employees she manages and developing personal relationships with senior management at client organizations. Carol is highly skilled at contract negotiations with complex accounts.

Currently, Carol is Director of Business Development for the **Princeton Center for Education (PCES)** focusing on developing new vertical markets for PCES's software solutions. Additionally, Carol works with industry leaders on a consulting basis to increase sales revenue, provide interim marketing and sales support, and other executive functions. Prior to PCES, Carol was the Senior Vice President - Sales and Marketing for ARGI, a privately owned company that sold software solutions to the publishing industry. Before ARGI, Carol was Vice President of Sales at Getty Images, a leading provider of digital media content and imagery worldwide. In the telecom sector, Carol held executive level positions with P&L responsibility at AT&T and AT&T Broadband (now Comcast) from 1995 to 2003. Carol earned her BA from Brandeis University, an MA from Columbia University, and her MBA from the Stern School of Business at New York University. In her spare time, Carol is passionate about "giving back" and is on the Board of Cherub Improv, a NYC-based non-profit organization, and assisting the Union Settlement Association with its fundraising efforts.

Contents

Preface

One of the most important decisions you'll make as a manager—and you'll be making it again and again, on a daily basis—is how best to approach and deal with your employees.

Too often, this is a decision that is made by default: managers, especially new ones, don't so much decide on a management style as fall into one, without giving the question much thought: they simply act toward their employees in a way that's comfortable and convenient for them, in keeping with their personalities, or perhaps by modeling themselves on a manager they've worked under in the past. (Some even mimic their parents!)

But this is a big mistake. How you interact with your staff, and indeed with other employees in your organization, will be a major determinant of your success as a manager. It will impact how your employees behave, how they perform, and how they perceive you; and it will go a long way toward determining how your superiors perceive you as well. Your success as a manager depends to a very great extent to how you deal with the question of management style. You should be thinking hard about this question, not simply allowing it to happen to you.

This book will help you to understand the key elements of management style, how to decide when to use each one, and what the advantages and disadvantages of each approach are. By the time you're done reading, you will be the sort of manager who approaches each situation with thought and foresight, rather than one who just stumbles into things.

Conventions

In this book, you will find a number of styles of text that distinguish between different kinds of information. Here are some examples of these styles, and an explanation of their meaning.

New terms and **important words** are shown in bold.

Make a note
Warnings or important notes appear in a box like this.

Tip
Tips and tricks appear like this.

Reader feedback

Feedback from our readers is always welcome. Let us know what you think about this book—what you liked or may have disliked. Reader feedback is important for us to develop titles that you really get the most out of.

To send us general feedback, simply send an e-mail to `contact@impacktpub.com`, and mention the book title via the subject of your message.

If there is a book that you need and would like to see us publish, please send us a note via the **Submit Idea** form on `https://www.impacktpub.com/#!/bookidea`.

Piracy

Piracy of copyright material on the Internet is an ongoing problem across all media. At Packt, we take the protection of our copyright and licenses very seriously. If you come across any illegal copies of our works, in any form, on the Internet, please provide us with the location address or website name immediately so that we can pursue a remedy.

Please contact us at `copyright@impacktpub.com` with a link to the suspected pirated material.

We appreciate your help in protecting our authors, and our ability to bring you valuable content.

Why Management Style Matters

People don't always stop to think about the question of the precise role and purpose of a manager. They think it's obvious, so they don't bother to articulate it, or even to think about it much.

Actually, though, if you ask most managers, they'd be unlikely to zero in on the one thing that should in fact be guiding their thinking as managers:

The role of a manager is to maximize the performance of the people who report to him or her, in order best to achieve the objectives of the organization.

Take a close look at the preceding statement, and think about its implications. What does it say about how managers should conduct themselves, and about management style?

Many managers, especially new ones, take the position that they're the boss and that it's up to their employees to adapt themselves to the manager's preferred way of doing things; that managers have their own styles and preferences, and everyone needs to adapt accordingly.

But how likely is that approach to lead to optimal performance on the part of employees? For example, if a certain employee does excellent work by organizing the work on his or her own, does it really make sense for a manager to step in and tell the employee to organize it some other way; the way in which the manager used to do it before becoming a manager? Is this likely to produce the best work of which that employee is capable? Will it motivate that employee and increase loyalty? In a case like this, it makes more sense for the manager to adapt to the employee, rather than the other way around.

Tip
Rule # 1 about being a manager: It's not about you!

Why style matters

Understanding the various management styles is crucially important to managerial success because it allows the thoughtful manager to choose the right style for each employee, circumstance, type of work, and environment. If you are to maximize your effectiveness as a manager, you must be able to apply the appropriate managerial approach in each situation.

Tip
Your key task is to develop the ability to adapt your style to the nature of the employee and the situation.

There's another reason why style matters: it goes a long way toward determining the atmosphere of your office and the way employees interact and communicate with you. Your style says a lot about how you view your employees and what you expect of them, and will do much to shape their perceptions of you.

The elements of management style

Management styles have several aspects. Some academic taxonomies of management styles get very complicated by mixing up the different elements in various combinations and giving each combination an abstruse name, but it's best to think of management styles in terms of their various elements, and then to combine the elements yourself.

When managing any employee or situation, you should always be thinking of all of these elements.

Two axes

The most important elements of management style, and the ones that will do the most to define your approach in the eyes of others, are the two axes of:

> ➤ **Direction** versus **Consultation**

> ➤ **Control** versus **Autonomy**

The direction/consultation axis refers to the extent to which you keep decision-making to yourself and the extent to which you invite input from others.

The control/autonomy axis refers to the extent to which you determine how people should do their jobs and the extent to which you allow them to choose their own approach.

Guidance

The amount of guidance you provide your employees is another key element of management style. Guidance comes in three main forms:

> ➤ Coaching

> ➤ Mentoring

> ➤ Support

Coaching refers to the formal steps you take to develop an employee's skills in certain areas. These could be hard job skills, or soft skills such as communication or interpersonal skills.

Mentoring is a broader process, usually informal but sometimes formalized, whereby a more senior employee helps a less senior employee advance his or her career in various ways.

Support refers to steps you take less formally to help an employee along. These can include dealing with concrete issues, such as addressing obstacles that may have been created by other areas of the company and that make it difficult for your employee to get the work done, and softer issues, such as a lack of confidence on the part of the employee.

Orientation

The final main element of management style is orientation. This is the extent to which you manage in the interests of the organization as opposed to those of the employee. Although it may sound obvious that you are hired to serve the needs of the organization, dealing with people is never that simple.

Adapt!

The key point about these various styles—and if you take one thing away from this book, make it this—is that it's crucial for you to develop the ability to adapt the approach you take, depending on the circumstances. Different people, with different personalities and different levels of experience need to be managed in different ways; and different types of work, done in different types of companies or other institutions, also requires different approaches.

Make a note

Being able to adapt your management style to suit the people you're working with and the circumstances in which you're working with them is a core management skill. Developing this skill will be crucial to your success.

This point is especially true in today's world, where highly educated knowledge workers, and young people raised on social media, will not mesh well with a rigid and inflexible managerial style.

Managing on a spectrum

It's also important to understand that the management styles mentioned above are not rigid "either/or" choices. Each one is, in general, a spectrum. For example, when you're looking at the direction/consultation axis, you don't decide which of those two poles you're going to choose; you decide where on a continuum you're going to come down.

Direction ———————————————— Consultation

You may choose to be highly directive, or highly consultative; but you may also choose to be a bit of both. You can approach a given person or situation from any point on the spectrum.

In the case of coaching and support, the spectrum is more a question of degree; you may offer a given employee a lot of coaching, or you may offer very little. As always, it's a question of adapting appropriately to circumstances.

No coaching ———————————————— Lots of coaching

Like the two axes, orientation is a spectrum; you'll continually be moving back and forth along a continuum between the interests of the employee and those of the organization.

Employee ———————————————— Organization

Managing work versus managing people

One final point before we start to dig into the meat and potatoes. It's worthwhile to make a distinction between managing work and managing people. Managing work is actually pretty easy; it's mostly a question of being organized and of keeping on top of deadlines. In today's environment, though, you rarely have the luxury of simply managing work; you have to manage people as well. Managers who step into a management role thinking that it's just a question of getting the work done are riding for a fall; you have to be prepared to deal with the people side of things as well.

Incidentally, this is a mistake that people sometimes make when they're hiring: they hire someone who's really good at getting work done, thinking that this is a qualification for management. But the hard part of management is dealing with people. Never forget that. (By the way, sometimes people make the opposite mistake as well: they hire someone with people skills who's no good at the work. Needless to say, that doesn't work either.)

Case study: Dave and Rhonda

Let's talk about two employees who work in our organization, Dave and Rhonda.

Rhonda is a recent recruit, fresh out of university. She has a liberal arts degree, and she has a bit of work experience from when she was a student. She did three work terms in various types of office, including one that was pretty similar to ours; and during her class terms she worked as a waitress in a restaurant and behind the counter at a coffee bar. She also volunteered in the University library and with disadvantaged children.

Dave is in his early fifties, and is a senior engineer. He has been with our firm for 26 years. Although he is considered highly skilled and competent by both his colleagues and his superiors, he has never expressed any interest in management, and the higher-ups also see him more as an individual contributor than as a manager. Although his interpersonal skills are perfectly satisfactory for doing his job, he doesn't consider himself to be much of a "people person", and he's not hugely interested in the people side of the job, or of anything else for that matter.

As you progress through this book, Dave and Rhonda will appear in various situations and contexts, and you will be asked to think about how you, as their manager, should respond. Although there are no absolutely right answers for this sort of thing, some suggestions as to how you might want to act will be provided at the end of each chapter.

Summary

In this chapter, you have:

> - Considered the nature of the manager's role
> - Learned about the key role management style plays in determining the success of you and your team
> - Considered the importance of adaptability
> - Distinguished between managing work and managing people
> - Met our two case study employees, Dave and Rhonda

Now let's take a closer look at the first element of management style, the direction/consultation axis.

The Elements of Management Style: Direction versus Consultation

One of the main features of your management style in any given situation will be where you place yourself on the direction/consultation axis.

The answer you provide to this question will go a long way toward shaping your relationship with your employees.

Case study: Dave and Rhonda

You and your team have been informed that the building you're located in has been sold, and that your department will be relocating to one of the company's other locations. Your superiors have asked for your input as to where you would prefer to go. There's space available in several locations, one of which is quite close to your home, though it's less convenient for Dave and Rhonda.

How should you handle this? (We'll come back to this at the end of the chapter.)

What is the direction/consultation axis?

The direction/consultation axis is the degree to which you take input from your subordinates in decision-making and on other questions impacting the running of your department.

Highly directive managers do their own analysis, make decisions on their own, and tell employees how things are going to be.

Consultative managers listen to people's ideas and analysis, hear their thoughts about how to proceed in various circumstances, and take their views into account.

This is not to say that the boss relinquishes control over decision-making or is obliged to accept the suggestions of others; the person responsible to the higher-ups is always the one who has the final say. But a consultative manager hears what others have to say, takes their perspectives into account, and then sifts the wheat from the chaff.

Managing on the direction/consultation spectrum

As we discussed in the first chapter, it's important to remember that the direction/consultation axis is a spectrum or continuum, and not just two poles. In any situation, you need to decide where on the continuum you want to position yourself. Different scenarios—and different employees—will necessitate a different mix or balance between the two poles.

Direction ——————————————— Consultation

As a general rule, it's better to hear what people have to say unless you've got a good reason not to. In other words, consult whenever you can; don't be directive unless you have to be.

Choosing between them

How do you know when you should be more directive and when you should be more consultative? There's no simple formula; every situation is different, and every situation is complex. Having said that, though, here are a few rules of thumb.

Consider being more **directive** when:

> ➤ You have a tightly defined objective that has to be met
>
> ➤ You have a tight deadline
>
> ➤ You have a lot more knowledge and experience than the group
>
> ➤ You're dealing with an individual who just needs or wants a lot of direction and is not comfortable with independent thought or action
>
> ➤ You're in a high-turnover environment, such that employees don't stay around long enough to develop real experience and you're not concerned about integrating them into a strong, cohesive team
>
> ➤ The stakes are high and you simply don't have a lot of faith in the group's analytical abilities

Consider being more **consultative** when:

> ➤ Your employees do work that is highly specialized in nature and therefore know things you don't
>
> ➤ Your team is competent and mature, and has valuable things to contribute
>
> ➤ You want to build team cohesion
>
> ➤ You have people who are suitable for advancement
>
> ➤ Your employees have more experience than you do
>
> ➤ You're dealing with an issue that impacts some employees closely
>
> ➤ Pretty much all the time; as a general rule, it's better to include people unless there's a legitimate reason not to

The impact on employees

Why is it important to think about your management style so much? Because the style you choose will have a major impact on your office, in two different ways. It will impact the quality of the work done, and it will impact the attitude of your employees toward both you and the organization at large.

The work

It's been said before: two heads are better than one. When you get the perspectives of other people, and hear their ideas and their thoughts, you're far more likely to make good decisions. Good decision-making relies on gathering a lot of information and considering a lot of alternative courses of action. This is far more likely to happen if you take input from several thoughtful people. There are very few people who have all the answers themselves (although there are some). Remember that it's always possible for you to miss something. Your employees have a ground-level perspective and hands-on experience with the work and the clients, which you, as a manager, may lack; they almost certainly have something useful to say.

As implied previously, however, there is a caveat that needs to be mentioned: if your people are really not very insightful, or if they consistently come up with ideas that are unworkable or inefficient, consulting with them may be little more than an exercise in public relations, or indeed completely useless. You have to decide whether such a PR exercise is worth undertaking. In such a situation, doing things on your own may be more worthwhile.

The attitude of the employees

Managerial styles convey messages to employees, and they go a long way toward setting the tone of the office.

A directive style tends to make people feel as though they're regarded as disposable objects. They do not feel valued; their thoughts and experience seem not to be respected. Their loyalty to you and to the organization is unlikely to be strong if they do not feel heard.

A consultative style, on the other hand, sends the opposite messages: people's ideas are valued and respected; their thoughts and the other fruits of their experience and abilities are worth hearing. A consultative approach to management can be highly motivating and can instill considerable loyalty in employees. This is particularly true when you're consulting them about matters that impact them significantly. A consultative approach is also a good way to build up the cohesion of the team.

It's also worth noting that a consultative style can help people feel that you and your workplace are inclusive and non-hierarchical. Most people prefer such a workplace, and in this day and age in particular, people, especially young people, expect to have a voice. Hierarchy is passé; forward-looking environments are open and non-hierarchical.

Make a note

Being directive distances you from your employees and sends the message that you don't think their thoughts have value. It closes down communication, because people don't talk if they're told that what they have to say is not of interest.

Being consultative brings people together. People will talk to you and keep you informed of things you should know about if they feel that you're open to what they have to say.

Risks

You have to be careful of being overly directive with people who are capable, and who are able to contribute at a higher level than what you're allowing them. Such a person will become disaffected very quickly, and is likely to seek other employment. Remember also that an overly directive environment is unlikely to be a pleasant one; it is more likely to be one that causes people to wish they were somewhere else. And 'pulling rank' simply to gain an advantage for yourself will send a very hostile message. Finally, as noted above, being excessively directive can cause you to make decisions on the basis of partial or incomplete information, as you may be missing key insights and perspectives that other people may have.

Being overly consultative also carries risks. It can create the impression in people's minds that the workplace is more of a democracy than it actually is; a certain sort of person sometimes gets the idea that he or she is the one in charge. And if not done correctly, it can create the impression that the manager is too dependent on others, and maybe lacks confidence or knowledge.

Also, excessive consultation can lead to endless meetings and can slow down decision-making. Ideally, consultation should be tightly focused: when possible, ask for people's input on a clearly defined question. Ask specific questions as to what they have experienced or perceived, and possibly about what they think should be done; and only ask those who are actually in a position to bring something useful to the conversation.

Remember also that there will be occasions when you have to make a decision without consulting your team, or in disregard of their input. This can put people's noses out of joint; but in such cases, explaining your reasons for the decision can go a long way toward healing any rift that opens up. (Note that this of course implies that you have good, solid reasons for your decision.)

Case study: Dave and Rhonda

How would you handle the situation outlined at the beginning of the chapter? You could be directive, of course, and pull rank on them to ensure that your own convenience was met; but this would send a very bad message. It would tell the others that they don't matter and are not valued, and it would build a wall between them and you, and between them and the organization. It is quite likely to make them feel downright hostile toward you and the company.

The best solution would be to sit down with them, consider the options, and try to find a solution that's fair to everyone. You don't have to sacrifice your own convenience to maximize theirs; an effort to find a fair compromise that takes everyone's point of view into account sends the message that you're all colleagues, that everyone's concerns and interests deserve to be treated with respect, and that your office doesn't enforce hierarchy pointlessly. It will greatly increase the respect with which your employees regard you, and it will increase their loyalty to you and to the company, as well as their willingness to communicate with you and to approach you about issues that may arise.

In a situation such as this, though, it will often be the case that there are winners and losers: the final decision is likely to be closer to what some people want than to what others want. To minimize this effect, other aspects of the problem can often be considered during the decision-making process. In our example, factors such as availability of public transport, proximity to a highway, plentiful parking—anything that can make for an easier commute—could be taken into account during the discussion, to mitigate the harm to those who may not be as close to the new location as they'd like. Consultation can involve negotiation.

Note also that there may be situations where you would want to consult with some employees but not others. If there were an issue that directly touched on the engineering aspect of the work, consulting with Dave but not Rhonda would be entirely reasonable. You may also want to bring someone like Dave in on other aspects of the running of the department, due to his seniority, competence, and experience. This would give him some status in the department and give him a feeling of acknowledgment.

Finally, as noted above, it's important that both you and your employees understand that consultation does not create an obligation in you to act on their advice. It is you who are ultimately responsible, and therefore it is you who must have the final say. You should, however, listen seriously and sincerely to their input on matters on which it is appropriate for you to consult them.

Make a note

Being directive for your own convenience sends a message of contempt to your employees, and is likely to be demotivating and to engender hostility towards you and the company. Your bosses will notice this, too.

Summary

In this chapter, you have:

- ➤ Been introduced to the direction/consultation axis
- ➤ Learned when to choose direction and when to choose consultation
- ➤ Considered the impact on employees of each style
- ➤ Learned about the risks of getting it wrong

Now let's take a look at the control/autonomy axis.

3

The Elements of Management Style: Control versus Autonomy

The second of the two main management-style axes is the control/autonomy axis.

As is the case with the direction/consultation axis, your relationship with your employees will be shaped to a significant extent by how you place yourself on this axis.

Case study: Dave and Rhonda

You have a small but important engineering project that you need Dave to do, and it needs to be done fairly quickly. He has no problem with doing it, but his son is off school, and his wife is traveling for her own work. He was planning on working from home for a few days, but our company discourages employees from working on such projects from home, for quality control reasons. Because of the importance of the project, he also needs to complete a technical report on it when he's done; the report will be seen by senior management in the company, and needs to follow a certain format.

As for Rhonda, she is currently learning a new process that will be her responsibility on an ongoing basis. She heard Dave mention that he wanted to work at home because of his son, and says that she would also like to work at home. She says that since the process she's learning just involves her working on her own at her desk, and since she's fully connected to the office, it should not be a problem.

How much autonomy would you give Dave and Rhonda in these cases, and how much control would you exert?

What is the control/autonomy axis?

The control/autonomy axis refers to the amount of control you exert over how employees do their jobs and the degree to which you allow employees to make those decisions themselves, and thus to have autonomy over their own activities.

As such, the control/autonomy axis is not unrelated to the direction/consultation axis. Both relate to the question of who has the power to determine how things are done. Direction/consultation pertains to general decision-making regarding projects, strategy, solutions to problems and so on; control/autonomy pertains to how each person approaches his or her own job tasks.

It should not be assumed, therefore, that a high degree of direction automatically implies a high degree of control. A manager could be highly directive as to how an issue is to be approached—what the deadlines are, what the strategy should be, what the goals or targets are, and so forth—while at the same time ceding full autonomy to employees in actually getting it all done. Direction and control is not the same thing, and it is perfectly possible for a manager to give a lot of direction and a lot of autonomy simultaneously.

Note also that giving your employees some autonomy doesn't mean that you shouldn't still keep an eye on things. You should always be evaluating performance and making sure that things are done well. But if you see employees doing things differently from how you would have done them, try to be open to their ideas.

Tip

Push decision-making down to the lowest level that is capable of doing it. As a general rule, decisions should be pushed down to the lowest-level employees capable of making them. This allows the people who are closest to the situation in question to determine how to handle it. It also increases efficiency by reducing the amount of time that managers are spending on things that people at lower levels could be handling.

Managing on the control/autonomy spectrum

Like the direction/consultation axis, the control/autonomy axis is a continuum. The situation and the people you're dealing with will determine where on the spectrum you choose to place yourself.

Control ———————————— Autonomy

Tip

Autonomy is generally better than control. Very few people want or need to be micro-managed (although there are a small number who do).

Choosing between control and autonomy

Again, there are no firm rules as to how to decide how much control is needed in a given situation. The following list has a few suggestions, however.

Consider being more **controlling** when:

➤ You're managing a well-defined process that needs to be followed exactly and carefully

➤ You have a tight deadline

➤ You're dealing with an employee who is very new, or one who needs to learn how to do the job correctly

➤ You're dealing with an employee who prefers to be managed very closely

➤ You're not sure an employee won't take advantage of autonomy to goof off and not do much of anything

➤ You don't feel that your team is all that talented, and you don't feel comfortable giving them a lot of autonomy

Consider allowing more **autonomy** when:

➤ Your employees are mature and capable and know what they're doing

➤ Whenever you can; don't be controlling unless you have a firm reason to be

The impact on employees

Your choice between control and autonomy will have effects upon the work and the attitudes of employees.

The work

Most of the time, your employees will have ground-level knowledge of the work and of your clients. This means that they should be able to determine the best way to approach the work. Allowing them to determine on their own how things should be done will usually lead to good results. (This of course assumes an appropriate level of competence in the employees in question.)

The attitude of the employees

With few exceptions, people prefer to have control over their own lives as much as possible. They much prefer to work in an environment where they have a degree of autonomy.

Autonomy is a great motivator. Research has shown that simply allowing people to make their own decisions, where possible, increases involvement, motivation, and work satisfaction. It thus increases loyalty and aids employee retention.

Tip
As a general rule, give people autonomy unless you have a good reason not to.

Risks

Just as people prefer to have autonomy in their work-lives, they generally abhor people who try to control them. If you take an unnecessarily controlling approach, employees will be unhappy and unmotivated, and they simply won't want to work for you. Higher-level decision-makers will look at your employees' attitudes toward you when they're evaluating you.

Controlling people too much conveys the message that you don't trust them or that you don't think they're competent; it makes them feel as though they're being treated like children. It also makes you seem uptight and lacking in confidence.

On the other hand, you also have to remember that not all employees like or want autonomy, or do well when they have it. A small number of people want or need to be highly managed. You need to be able to identify these people. There's nothing wrong with asking people how they feel about this, if you feel you need to.

By the same token, new employees or those with little experience are unlikely to be able to handle as much autonomy as others. You should always be judging the amount of autonomy each individual employee can handle.

Another risk is that, if you give a lot of autonomy to people, there is a possibility that they will abuse it. They may set things up to make their own lives easier, for example, rather than to maximize value to the organization or to the customer. The purpose of giving them autonomy is to allow them most effectively to apply their skills and experience to the goal of coming up with the best solutions and the best work possible for the organization and its clients.

Don't make the mistake of going overboard with the autonomy either. If you go out of your way to tell people how much you trust them and how capable they are, and you just let them decide everything in an effort to get them to like you, they will lose respect for you, and you will lose control of the work. You should never carry autonomy to the point where anything goes, and where you never say anything to anyone out of fear that they won't like you.

Managers who are responsible for hiring managers should also think carefully about the nature of the people they are considering for management positions. People with highly controlling natures often find it difficult to cede control; and changing their behaviors and attitudes is almost impossible, because this kind of rigidity is a deep-seated personality issue. Such people can be very difficult to work for, and many people—especially independent thinkers and creative types—will be unwilling to accept them as managers. Such managers do best in environments that actually require high levels of control, and detailed, accurate work. Otherwise, think twice before putting them in charge of other people.

Case study: Dave and Rhonda

Given Dave's experience and track record of high-quality work, and his proven maturity, skill, and competence, there is no reason not to allow him a high degree of autonomy: he knows how to do the work, and he doesn't need someone telling him how to do it. The company's stricture against working from home is expressed as a preference, and concerns quality issues; this is a pretty clear-cut case where this preference can be ignored. Dave's record makes it highly unlikely that quality will be an issue, and he has a good reason for wanting to work from home. You can always check the work for quality later, if necessary.

The report, on the other hand, is a different matter. It needs to be done a certain way, and it's going to the higher-ups. As such, it will reflect on you at least as much as it reflects on Dave. Furthermore, on the basis of the limited amount of information we have about him, Dave's communication skills may not be all that great, and he may not take a report of this sort all that seriously. In this case, you'll want to either work closely with him on the preparation of the report, or review it carefully when he's drafted it, requesting any revisions that you think are needed. You'll need to exercise more control here than you do on the project itself.

As for Rhonda, she's inexperienced and is just learning a process that she will be performing on an ongoing basis. She should be supervised and instructed as she's learning, and steps should be taken to ensure that she's learning to do this work in the best way possible.

As far as working from home goes, this mostly depends on her reliability and on the organization's views on working from home for work of the type she's doing, as well as on your ability to supervise and instruct at distance. There's no need for her to work from home, but if you think you can trust her, and if the organization encourages working from home in such cases, and if you can monitor her appropriately while she does so, you could at least consider it.

Remember that your decision-making in such cases should always take into account not just the employee you're dealing with, nor just the specific situation you're facing, but both simultaneously. Employees always exist in the context of a situation; you can't separate the two.

Summary

In this chapter, you have learned:

- ➤ A definition of the control/autonomy axis
- ➤ When to choose control and when to choose autonomy
- ➤ The impact on employees of each style
- ➤ The risks attendant on getting it wrong

Let's move on now to a consideration of the different forms of guidance you can offer your employees.

The Elements of Management Style: Coaching, Mentoring, and Supporting

Another key element of management style is the amount of guidance you offer your employees, and the way in which you offer it. Broadly speaking, there are three ways of offering guidance:

➤ Coaching

➤ Mentoring

➤ Support

Some managers feel that this sort of thing is not their problem, but you'll be a much more effective manager if you adopt these roles when it's appropriate for you to do so.

Case study: Dave and Rhonda

Dave has been working on an engineering project for another department in the organization, but you've been getting complaints from the other department that they never know what's going on with the project, despite their attempts to get information from Dave. When you asked the other department how Dave has been responding to their requests for information, they showed you some e-mails he sent; they're brief, and not very informative.

Rhonda just got a phone call from her mother saying that her father has been taken to hospital due to a heart attack; and she's not taking the news too well.

What should you do?

Coaching

What is coaching?

There are many different types of coaching, but workplace coaching between a manager and an employee usually involves a formal process of instruction and guidance that is directed toward a specific goal, generally the learning by the employee of a new skill or behavior, or improvement in an existing one. These can be hard, job-related skills, such as learning a process or the use of new software, or soft skills, such as interpersonal skills.

When to coach

Use coaching when you have an employee who has a specific, well-defined gap in terms of a skill that is needed for the job or a behavior that needs to be exhibited in the workplace. The following are a few examples:

> ➤ A new employee has to learn a process to follow
>
> ➤ An employee has to use new software for the first time
>
> ➤ An employee speaks too harshly to people and alienates them
>
> ➤ An employee is more or less ready for promotion, but has specific gaps that need to be filled

How to coach

When you're coaching an employee, it's a good idea to have a plan. The starting point is to have a clear and precise definition of the skill that the employee needs to develop.

You should then plan and schedule coaching sessions that will lead the employee toward the goal. Meet regularly to review progress since the last meeting and to define what needs to be achieved before the next one.

Don't try to get the employee fully up to speed in a single go; break the task into steps and define milestones. Find ways to monitor the employee's progress and to determine when the desired goal has been reached. Ideally, come up with a definition of success and of completion of the task.

Coaching is a collaboration

Remember that coaching should be collaborative, not directive. The manager and the employee are working together to achieve a goal. The input, ideas, and perspective of the employee are important. It should not be treated as a punishment or a top-down exercise.

This implies that there needs to be buy-in on the part of the employee. If you have a situation where you're coaching an employee because you feel that there's a problem that needs to be addressed but the employee does not feel that a problem exists, you may need to do some work to make the employee aware of the issue before coaching can begin. As a general rule, coaching is far more effective when the employee is on board.

Non-managerial coaching

Finally, remember that there are other types of coaching that managers would not normally do themselves. Professional coaches generally work on broader questions of general outlook and mindset, attitudes toward life, balancing work and home life, and so on. If you feel that an employee has issues of this sort that are affecting their work, you may want to refer that employee to an appropriate coach.

Mentoring

What is mentoring?

Mentoring is a broader, more general process of guidance whereby a more experienced individual helps a person take the necessary steps to develop in and advance his or her career. Although this may include some coaching, it more often focuses on analysis and advice, and on helping the person being mentored by sharing contacts, providing introductions to people to whom the junior person may not otherwise have access, or putting in a good word for the employee with people in a position to offer assistance or employment.

Although managers sometimes try to act as mentors, and employees sometimes try formally to get senior people in their organizations to act as mentors – and some companies set up formal mentoring programs – this is not always particularly successful, because a true mentoring relationship is a much more personal one than the average manager-employee relationship or than that which results when a senior person is paired with a less senior one. As such, mentoring tends to work best when it grows naturally, as opposed to in a calculated way, out of a genuine personal relationship between a more and a less experienced person. While it's always good for managers and employees to have a good relationship, it's unlikely that their relationship will be such that a true mentoring relationship will arise.

When to mentor

Act as a mentor with someone:

- ➤ Who wants to be mentored
- ➤ With whom you have a good relationship that goes beyond the cordial nature of a workplace relationship
- ➤ Whose goals and objectives you understand well and are able to advance
- ➤ Who has substantially less experience and knowledge than you, and who could perhaps benefit from your contacts

How to mentor

Mentoring can be done in different ways. You may want to set up regular meetings to discuss various issues, or you may want to meet informally from time to time. A lot depends on the situation and the relationship between the two parties. Mentoring activities can include:

- ➤ Providing general advice around specific issues and situations that arise
- ➤ Providing advice about long-term career goals and direction
- ➤ Providing information about how an organization works and who the key players are
- ➤ Developing a plan to prepare for advancement; determining training to take, skills to learn, departments to work in or learn about
- ➤ Attitude adjustment, where necessary
- ➤ Making introductions to useful people

Support

What do we mean by support?

Support is used here as a broader term for the less focused types of non-skills-related input you may need to offer employees from time to time. For example, an employee may be having trouble getting work done because of some unbreakable bureaucratic blockage within your organization, and may need your assistance to work around this. Or an employee may not be doing as well as possible due to a lack of confidence or self-esteem that makes going all-in to maximize performance difficult for that individual. You may need to find a way to build up that employee's confidence. Occasionally, you may need to buck a person up regarding a personal issue that has nothing to do with work in itself but that impacts performance nonetheless.

Some managers may feel uncomfortable offering this latter kind of support, or they may think that it's not really part of their job; and this is understandable. But these issues can have a big effect on how employees do their jobs, so it's not a bad idea to be thinking about this sort of thing; and if you want to be a truly effective manager who maximizes the team's performance, you should certainly be looking at your employees holistically and considering all aspects of each person's "work-self" to see how, and whether, you can help.

When to offer support

You should offer support on an as-needed and as-wanted basis, ad hoc. Try to be aware of obstacles that are facing your employees in getting their work done. Obstacles can be of different kinds:

> ➤ An employee doesn't have the necessary tools or equipment for the job
> ➤ Outside forces, such as other departments, are failing to provide information, materials, or the right conditions to allow your employee to get the work done
> ➤ An employee has a certain mindset or attitude that inhibits success, such as a fear of failure
> ➤ An employee has personal issues that impact their work

The type of response you provide will of course vary depending on the situation. If there is a problem with another area of your company, interceding with that department should be fairly straightforward. If, on the other hand, the problem is of a more personal nature, a high degree of sensitivity is required. You have to decide how to approach the situation, and whether it's even appropriate for you to do so. It may be necessary to discuss the matter with your Human Resources department.

Risks

The biggest risk here is that you put your foot in something sensitive and handle it badly. Never make assumptions about what another person is feeling; ask first. Then address the problem directly, as it relates to the job. If, for example, the person is feeling a lack of confidence, a simple pep talk may help; show the employee that they have done well in the past, and give objective reasons as to why you feel that you can have faith in them.

If, on the other hand, the person is dealing with some serious personal issue, focus exclusively on how it impacts work and how you can help get the work done (assuming that there's not a case for giving the employee some time off while other team-members cover the work). Don't try to offer life advice; the odds that you're even remotely qualified are almost nil, and the risk of doing some real damage is high. Hand this one off to the HR department, or tell the person about your organization's **Employee Assistance Program (EAP)**, if it has one.

Think also about how much support the person actually wants. Some employees will like the idea of a highly supportive manager and environment, whereas some may find it intrusive: some people prefer to sort things out on their own. Some may not want to discuss a sensitive or personal topic with you. An older employee may not want to discuss certain issues with a much younger manager. You only have an absolute right to get involved to the extent that there's an impact on the work or on the functioning of the office. Otherwise, though, you should do your best to be sensitive to the preferences of employees.

Another risk is simply that you miss something. Try to be aware of how things are going with your employees. The best managers have insight into people and an awareness of both their personalities and their states of minds. It's not easy to learn this type of awareness; do your best to be sensitive and to use your head.

Case study: Dave and Rhonda

Dave needs some coaching on how to communicate when dealing with his internal clients. Set up some meeting time and explain to him what's been going on, and explain why the e-mails he sent would be unclear to people in another group. Define what good communication looks like, and set up a communication plan with him so that he has clear steps to follow in communicating with others. (This could be a schedule according to which he will update them and specific points of information that he will provide.) Schedule a few regular appointments to see how things are going and to ensure that everything is on track. Remember to take his input throughout.

Rhonda needs some support in dealing with her father's heart attack. Ask her what you can do for her. Let her know that she is free to go down to the hospital right away. Most organizations allow some time off to deal with situations of this sort; see what you can do to help her out. Tell her she can call in at the end of the day to discuss taking some time off if she wants. If possible, see if there's someone available to make the trip to the hospital with her, if she feels she wants some support.

Summary

In this chapter, you have learned:

> ➤ When it's appropriate to offer coaching, and how to do it

> ➤ How to identify suitable candidates for mentoring

> ➤ What support is, and when to offer it

> ➤ The risks attendant on getting it wrong

We'll now move on to a consideration of the question of how to deal with the conflict between the interests of the organization and those of an employee.

>5

The Elements of Management Style: The Organization or the Employee?

One of the fundamental issues in people management, and one that tends to rear its ugly head over and over again, is the tension that always exists between the interests of the organization and those of the employee.

Most managers want to treat their employees well and give them a good work environment and career-development opportunities, but often the requirements of the organization stand in the way of doing what's best for the employees.

The way you respond to these conflicting pressures will go a very long way toward determining how you are perceived by your employees. The problem is compounded by the fact that one of the main determinants of what you will be allowed to do is the culture of your organization. Most organizations decide at a high level the extent to which they want to focus on employees rather than on the interests of the organization itself; your own ability to decide will therefore always be somewhat constricted.

Tip

New managers often think they have a lot of decision-making leeway, but in reality, their employees, their superiors, and other groups in their organization substantially constrict their freedom of action.

Note that it is often this orientation that determines whether or not a company is regarded as a good one to work for. Organizations – and managers – that focus more on their own interests are the ones who "don't care about their employees" and who "treat their employees like trash". The ones that do the opposite are discussed in terms of the development opportunities they offer, their cutting-edge HR programs, and their positive atmosphere.

Case study: Dave and Rhonda

Dave has requested training on a new project-management software package for engineering projects. Although he's not a project manager per se, he thinks it will make him more effective in his work.

Rhonda wants to take a course on office processes and procedures that she feels will help her advance past her current, relatively junior level.

Should these requests be approved?

The organization/employee spectrum

It should be noted that, like the other topics we have discussed, the question of organization versus employee orientation involves managing on a spectrum.

Employee ———————————————— Organization

Depending on the situation you're dealing with, the organization you're in, and to a lesser extent, the employee in question, you will have to decide where exactly on this spectrum you want to place yourself.

Remember that management does not involve deciding on one style and then sticking with it no matter what; it is a process of continual decision-making and adaptation to individual situations and people.

The interests of the organization

What are the interests of the organization? They vary somewhat according to the nature of the organization: a hospital's idea of what it's about is different from that of a regular for-profit business, for example. But regardless of the nature of your organization, it has, broadly speaking, two objectives:

➤ To get the work done when it needs to be done, and to meet the needs of its clients

➤ To maximize the value it gets for its expenditures, and to minimize those expenditures

While your organization has no choice but to temper its zeal in achieving these objectives due to the countervailing fact that employees who are treated like objects are unlikely to contribute much or to hang around for long, these objectives remain its guiding principles.

Differences between organizations

As suggested above, the way in which a given organization will pursue these objectives will vary according to the type of organization and the nature of the specific institution in question. As a general rule, a business will focus on maximizing profits; but some businesses are a lot more single-minded in their pursuit of this objective than others. By the same token, the above-mentioned hospital is not focused on profit, and while it also keeps an eye on its budgets, its attitude, or at least its atmosphere, is probably a bit different. The same applies to government offices.

But the main point is that while these organizations all have their own feel and their own approach, they all have their own interests as well, and they will always pursue them.

The interests of the employee

The employee's interests, on the other hand, are to some extent in conflict with those of the organization. Although employees have an interest in the success of the organization and generally act accordingly, they also have other interests: maximizing their pay; developing in and advancing their careers; taking time off work; devoting time and energy to their families; and so on.

They have interests outside of work: they want to be able to take some vacation time, even if there's a lot of work to be done; they want to be able to look after their children when they're sick; they like to spend time on non-work interests that they are passionate about.

Even within the office, they have interests that may conflict with those of the organization: they want the boss to spend money on training for them; they want a promotion; they want to work on things they're interested in rather than dull things that need to be done; they want to avoid an employee whom they dislike but with whom they may need to work; and so forth.

Striking the balance

The trick in all this, of course, is finding the right balance; and unfortunately, there's no formula for doing so. As a general rule, you will need to put the requirements of the organization first; beyond that, be as supportive of your employees as you can.

Tip

Do as much as you can for your employees without sacrificing the interests of the organization.

Many factors will come into decisions about where you want to place yourself on the organization/employee spectrum:

> ➤ The nature of your organization is likely to make a difference; the attitude of businesses toward employees is generally different from that of public sector and not-for-profit organizations, and some organizations have clear policies about things like promotions and time off where others are more fluid.

> ➤ Your organization's culture will also have an impact on your decision-making; there's often a generally accepted way of doing things, and what's acceptable in one organization or workgroup may not be acceptable in another one that's otherwise comparable.

> ➤ Availability of resources will of course be a determining factor: you will usually have limited resources, and you will often have to base decisions on this factor alone.

> ➤ You'll want to differentiate between employees. Those who are more valued by the organization, for whatever reason, may need more attention than those who are less so. It's perfectly acceptable to treat different employees differently in similar situations if you have a reason.

> ➤ The nature of the circumstance will also come into play. If a person has the death of someone close to deal with, for example, do your best to be as helpful as you can. Most organizations will turn a blind eye to a little bending of the rules in such a situation.

The impact on employees

Where you place yourself on the organization/employee spectrum will of course have a huge impact on the attitude of your employees toward both you and your organization.

If you consistently orient yourself toward the organization (which the culture of your organization and the expectations of your higher-ups may force you to do), you will find that your employees distrust you and lack loyalty. They will perceive the organization as a bad place to work.

If, on the other hand, employees have the feeling that you are doing what you can for them, their trust and loyalty will increase, as will the constructive communication that can flow from these things. They won't expect much, as they know what the realities are; but a manager's attitude toward employees is not hard to discern, and will determine the employees' attitudes toward the manager, and thus their behavior toward the manager: it can act as a powerful motivator, and affect the way they work and how hard they work. They will be more likely to go the extra mile in a crisis if they feel that their manager has their interests at heart, even if there's not always much that the manager can do for them.

Risks

The organization/employee spectrum is the quintessential expression of the squeeze in which lower- and mid-level managers often find themselves, caught as they are between their subordinates and their superiors.

They must always, of course, keep an eye on the interests of the organization that is paying their salary and on the goals of those above them who are more familiar with the bigger strategic picture.

Tip
Ensuring that subordinates understand the organization's higher-level goals is a good way of aligning them with the organization's interests.

Your superiors will obviously be concerned if they see that you are sacrificing their goals and interests in order to ingratiate yourself with your team. At the same time, your employees will see you as a pushover, and they will take advantage of you, which will only make things worse for you with your superiors.

On the other hand, if your employees see that you are routinely throwing them under the bus in order to ingratiate yourself with your bosses, they will distance themselves from you, and they will regard you with scorn, contempt, and even hatred. Their motivation and loyalty will plummet, the quality of their work will drop, they will be less open and less communicative with you, and they will not be there when you need them. Those with skills that are in high demand will seek work in more employee-friendly environments; others may quit as well. If your bosses see that people do not want to work for you, your career is likely to suffer.

Managing this balancing act is not easy. To the extent that a rule of thumb can be formulated, it is the one stated earlier in this chapter, which bears reiterating: your core focus must be the objectives and interests of the organization, but as long as those are satisfied, do as much for your employees as you think you can. They will take note.

Case study: Dave and Rhonda

The training-requests scenario outlined earlier in this chapter is more complex than it may at first appear.

A lot will depend on available resources. In hard times, training is often the first thing to go (which is not a good idea in itself), and if the organization has been cutting back on training, you may have no choice but to say no to both on the grounds that there's just no money for it.

Assuming there is at least some money, Dave's request may represent something of a dilemma. As a general principle, it's a good idea to do more for those employees you value more highly, and requests from a valued senior employee like Dave should be taken seriously. On the other hand, it's not clear that this course will be all that useful to him, or that his taking the course will benefit the company in any way. You must make an assessment of this. If you find that you have to say, essentially, that you don't think it's worth the money for him to take this course, it's also worth assessing his general state of satisfaction. If he seems disgruntled in some way, you may want to see if there's some other development he can do that will be of more value and that will keep him happy. If, on the other hand, he's generally happy, and he only suggested doing this course on a passing whim, you can probably just explain your concerns and let it go. Depending on the circumstances, you may also want to look into the possibility of having someone in the organization who already has the skills in question walk Dave through it.

With Rhonda, the considerations are similar. Her contribution is far less important, so keeping her happy is less of a concern. Furthermore, before investing money in her, you should try to assess the likelihood of her resigning for something better. The cost of the course will also be a factor. Again, the possibility of having someone else show her what she needs to know should be considered.

On the other hand, you may feel that she is bright and talented and is worth developing and making an effort to retain, and is thus worth spending some money on. It may be that the skills covered in the course are skills you could use in the department, and that it would be good to have someone trained on them. This of course will increase your inclination to approve Rhonda's request.

Remember also that with training, it's always a good idea to try to assess the quality of the course itself before sending employees; don't just accept that it's a good course simply because it exists, which is what most people do.

Summary

In this chapter, you have learned:

➤ A definition of the organization/employee spectrum

➤ The difference between the interests of the organization and those of the employee

➤ The factors that will influence how you orient yourself on this spectrum

➤ The impact on employees of the orientation you choose

➤ The risks attendant on getting it wrong

Let's take a look now at some of the differences between employees that will influence your approach to each one.

Differences Between Employees

An important factor that will help determine how you choose between the various approaches discussed in the previous chapters will be the specific nature of each individual employee. Different people need to be handled differently, and you should try to take their characters into account.

Remember that your primary task as a people manager is to bring the best work out of people that they are capable of doing, in order to meet the objectives of your group and your organization. Understanding the circumstances under which they work best will help you achieve that goal.

A successful manager has insight into people, and is able to assess their natures and their needs.

There are a lot of ways to define or categorize people and to distinguish between them. For our purposes, a relatively simple schema will do. We'll look at this question from four different perspectives:

- ➤ Experience levels
- ➤ Personality types
- ➤ Ways of working
- ➤ Creativity

Case study: Dave and Rhonda

Dave has asked that he be allowed to block off two solid days to get his head around a particular engineering problem that he says he needs to be able to focus on intently to resolve.

Rhonda has told you that she's finding it difficult to focus on her work because of the location of her desk, which is in a high-traffic area that exposes her to a lot of ambient noise. She wants to move to a quieter spot.

How will you respond to these requests?

Differentiating between employees

There are several factors that distinguish employees from one another.

Experience levels

The amount of experience an employee has is very likely to influence your approach. Normally, more experienced employees will be worth consulting with and will value their autonomy. They will generally require less direction and control. There will be fewer occasions where coaching and support are required.

By the same token, the less experienced employee is more likely to require direction, control, coaching, and support. Consulting with such an employee will, in general, be appropriate in certain circumstances, but probably not as often as with a more experienced person.

It should be noted, however, that these guidelines are far from absolute. There are plenty of experienced employees who need a lot of direction and coaching, and there are plenty of less experienced ones who are able to work very well with a high level of autonomy, and whose input is worth hearing.

The real point is to think about how you're going to handle each individual.

Tip

Employees with more experience need to be handled differently from those with less experience.

Personality types

Another thing to think about in this context is simply the sort of person each individual is, because this plays a substantial role in determining a person's work style. The topic of personality types is a big one, however, and could probably fill a book on its own; we can only make a few brief observations here.

Direction, control, coaching

Some people, by their nature, prefer more direction; they are uncomfortable making decisions or are inept at organizing work, and benefit greatly from a guiding hand. There are also people who simply don't tolerate highly controlling people and environments, and ideally should be allowed as much leeway as possible. Some people prefer to learn new things on their own, and some prefer to be coached. The point is that your insights into your employees' natures and effectiveness should guide your approach to managing each one.

Introverts and extraverts

Probably the biggest split in personality types is that between introverts and extraverts. Extraverts are more social and out-going, and are generally good at relationship-building and dealing with large groups. They tend not to go too in-depth with issues, and are less likely to take a point of view that's outside the mainstream, since their sociability often expresses itself as conformity. They're more comfortable with noisy environments and with frequent interruptions than introverts are.

Introverts, on the other hand, have many opposite skills. They can focus closely on problems and analyze them in detail; they listen well and take in the input of others; they plan well, and are more open to new ideas; they can be quite creative. They generally do best in quieter environments that allow them to focus closely on their work.

Problems tend to arise from the fact that introverts and extraverts rarely understand each other well, and this mutual incomprehension can often lead to dislike. It's well worth it for managers to take the time to understand their own orientation in this regard, and to make an effort to understand the opposite type; each type has skills that can be very valuable, and understanding this can lead to putting those skills to work in the best way possible. Managers should try to create the conditions in which their employees can do their best work, even if – or perhaps especially if – those employees are very different in nature from themselves.

Some managers and organizations use various psychological tests to try to understand employees, but there are some problems with this. One is that the accuracy and meaningfulness of such tests are questionable and that the tests are often pretty easy to game. Another is that if people are to work better together on the basis of the insights acquired from the tests, the results need to be followed up on and explored and an action plan needs to be implemented; and this is rarely done. It's difficult for people who are not trained psychologists to do it, or indeed to use these tests meaningfully at all.

Ways of working

Different people are successful working in different ways. Some do better working quietly on their own for hours, while others do better working on different things for short bursts. Some prefer to work with a partner or on a team.

Trying to impose a system on someone when it doesn't work for them will make that person less productive. Managers who make an effort to create the conditions that employees need to maximize their performance will themselves be more successful and will have a better rapport with their employees.

Tip

You can't change a person's nature. Creating conditions in which it is possible for employees to do their best work is far likelier to lead to a harmonious and productive workplace than trying to force them into a mold that doesn't fit.

Creative people

Creative people are in a class of their own; they too are a type who merit a much more detailed discussion than can be provided here. As a general rule, they are independent and analytical, and they often question everything. They are also, by definition, non-conformist. They thrive on autonomy and expect to be consulted. They challenge orthodoxy and question everything that's put to them.

It should be obvious by this point that control and direction won't work. These actually defeat the whole point of hiring creative thinkers.

Lots of managers say that they value creativity, but you should be sure that you're willing to accept the kind of person described above before you try to hire them. You should also be sure you know how to manage them if you do. Above all, you should be sure that you really want creative, original thinkers in your office, rather than those who will simply comply and conform.

The impact on employees

Taking the differences between your employees and their differing needs into account when you consider how best to manage them will make them more productive.

It will also make them a lot more comfortable working with you. It will give them the sense that you're open to their requirements and that you're willing to treat them with a certain respect. By making the workplace more congenial to their ways of working, you will make them more satisfied in their work, which will help with employee retention.

Risks

The main risk here is that you get it wrong: that you assess a person's needs incorrectly and thus manage that person incorrectly. There's an easy solution: talk to the person and find out what could be done differently to maximize performance.

Peripherally, there is another risk, which is that you try so hard to accommodate people that you end up jumping through hoops to keep them happy. Make sure that an employee's stated needs are legitimate, and that people are not just trying to take advantage of you. This is primarily a question of applying good judgment: think your employees' requests through. If you just accept everything they say, you're probably being led by the nose. By the same token, though, you shouldn't automatically reject everything they say, either.

There is of course a degree of risk in not thinking this question through at all; if you expect a high level of conformity to your own way of doing things, your employees will be less productive, less happy, less motivated, and less loyal.

Case study: Dave and Rhonda

Dave's request to block off two full days to work on his project is probably legitimate, though you may want to get a bit more information about precisely what it is he's doing. Unless there's some overwhelming reason why he needs to be available for other things, he should probably be left alone to do his work.

Rhonda's desire to move her desk is the kind of request that managers tend to abhor, for several reasons. For one thing, they're a pain in the neck; managers generally feel that they have enough on their plate and don't want to have to deal with things that may seem personal and trivial. They often feel that people should just take what they're given. For another, such requests can open the door to a lot of similar requests from other employees. Managers often brush them off out of hand.

But this can be a mistake. Rhonda's request sounds like the classic plea of an introvert not to be treated like an extravert. Introverts really do have trouble working in frantic environments, but they have a lot to contribute in terms of careful, detailed, thoughtful work. Trying to find Rhonda a more appropriate spot could pay solid dividends.

Of course, the possibility also exists that this is just a bit of jiggery-pokery. Maybe Rhonda, who's not very high up the totem pole, has been given a low-status spot to work in, and she's noticed a juicy location that she'd like to move to in order to stroke her ego. This of course would be a completely different situation.

Remember also that a more experienced or more valued employee would, in most cases, be approached with a different attitude from the one you might take with another employee, although there too your judgment of the individual's character and contributions will influence your responses.

Summary

In this chapter, you have:

➤ Learned the importance of understanding employees' differences

➤ Been introduced to some ways by which you can differentiate between employees

➤ Considered the impact on employees of your taking their different natures into account

➤ Examined the risks involved in miscalculating your managerial approach to a given employee

Now we'll conclude our consideration of management styles by looking at some key things that you should always be thinking about as a manager.

Conclusion: Things to Remember

Before we sign off, let's review the key concept of adaptability in a bit more detail.

We'll also touch on a couple of new points in this chapter, namely integrating appropriately with your team and dealing with your own personal issues.

Adaptability

It can never be emphasized enough: the most successful managers are the ones who are able to adapt their styles to the demands of the circumstances and the needs of their employees.

Tip

Being able to adapt your style to the demands of the situation you're facing is an essential skill to develop.

Adapting to the nature of your employees

The most important adaptations you will need to make are those that allow your employees to do their best work.

Remember that people have different natures and personalities, and that this has a substantial impact on how they work. Their personalities give them a "work style", just as managers need to develop a management style.

Having the insight to understand your employees' work styles and the flexibility to do what you can to allow them to act according to them will have several effects, chief among them that they will do better work, and that they will regard your office as a good place to be. Depriving people of their natural way of working makes them wish they were someplace else.

Adapting to the nature of the work

Different types of work require different approaches. If you're working on something that involves a certain process that needs to be followed closely, for example, you'll probably need to be more directive and controlling with your employees than if you're doing work where the only thing that matters is the quality of the end product, and where the way you get there isn't so important in itself.

Another case where more direction and control may be desirable is when your people are learning something new and you want to encourage certain best practices that may not be essential to the process but that will lead to better or more efficient work. Once you've shown them how it's done, however, you may need to let them choose how to apply what you've shown them.

Adapting to the needs of the organization

The way you deal with your employees, with the work your group is doing, and with various situations that arise will often be dictated by the broader needs of the organization. If times are lean and you are cutting back, you will not have the same leeway in dealing with your employees as you would in better times. If the organization has a specific business objective or an important client to please, your management style will need to reflect these targets.

It will be essential for you to adapt your interactions to the changing needs of your organization. While your superiors will want to see that you have a good relationship with your staff, their priority will of course be that you advance the interests of the organization. At the same time, employees who are not comfortable working for you will not do their best work and may leave altogether. As noted above, you will always be caught in this conflict to some extent. You'll need to be flexible and adaptable to deal with it.

Your place on the team

You should also be thinking about the nature of your relationship with the team. This too is a part of your management style.

Be part of the team

One of the best ways to alienate your personnel is to maintain a sharp line between you and them when it's not necessary to do so.

If you have a team event, such as a lunch, try to keep it relaxed. You're not working, so let your guard down a bit, and talk about other things than work. Handled properly, this will not impact your role as boss; it will enhance it.

If there's some sort of crisis that requires the team to work hard in order to resolve it, or if there's a very tight deadline to be met, roll up your sleeves and get in there with them to pitch in. Don't say "It's not my job", and take off.

Don't dump work. Delegate responsibly and appropriately. If there's some task that your team is responsible for but that no one likes, take a turn at it yourself every now and then.

Be tolerant of mistakes

If somebody makes a mistake of some sort or causes a screw-up, try to be tolerant and supportive. Chewing them out and dumping on them is rarely constructive, unless of course they do it all the time or the issue was the result of not really caring about the work. In the event of an honest mistake that happens once in a blue moon, the best response is to focus on cleaning up the mess. Pull the team together and do what's necessary to fix it; remember to pitch in yourself. Make people know that the team will support them to fix an error, because it's a fact of life that people make mistakes every now and then. Remember that it's only a question of time before you're the one who creates the problem and needs everyone's support to correct it.

After things are resolved, it's a good idea to try to figure out what went wrong (in a non-judgmental way) so that steps can be taken to avoid repeating the mistake. Unless there's some sort of ongoing problem with the individual in question, leave it at that and move on.

Your personal issues

Sometimes power goes to people's heads, even the little scrap of power involved in being a manager. Too often, managers, especially new managers, see being a manager as a license to give free rein to behavioral urges that were hitherto kept in check. This often boils down to using their employees as props to work out their own psychological issues, and this can take many forms:

> ➤ They treat employees as a captive audience when they're in the mood to drone on about what they did on the weekend or other aspects of their personal lives, and spend time during meetings and in other contexts indulging themselves in this way, without ever listening to what other people may have to say.

> ➤ They unconsciously model themselves on their parents in the way they interact with employees, and reenact the questionable behaviors their parents indulged in with them.

> ➤ They force a certain cherished image of themselves on employees, generally a completely fantastical one, and expect them to reinforce and validate their delusional, self-infatuated image of themselves.

> ➤ They stroke their own egos by subtly emphasizing their role as a superior in the organization, talking about conversations they had with higher-ups or drawing attention to some perk they get as a manager.

Obviously, this kind of conduct is completely inappropriate and unprofessional and should not be tolerated by senior management. Managers who behave in this way end up being regarded as buffoons by both their employees and their superiors.

Do your best to remember that management is not a power trip. You're there to do a job and to work constructively with your team, always in a professional and supportive way.

Tip
Rule #1 about being a manager: It's not about you!

Summary

In this chapter, you have:

- ➤ Reviewed the importance of adaptability
- ➤ Been introduced to some ways by which you can integrate well with the members of your team
- ➤ Considered the importance of keeping your personal issues away from the workplace

This concludes our introduction to management styles and our review of steps you can take to develop a successful approach to managing your team for maximum effectiveness. You should come back to this book from time to time to review the main points in order to make sure you're keeping on track.

Best of luck in your management career!

Harris Silverman